SUBJECT TO CHANGE
TRANS POETRY & CONVERSATION

SIBLING RIVALRY PRESS
LITTLE ROCK, ARKANSAS
DISTURB / ENRAPTURE

Sibling Rivalry Press, LLC
PO Box 26147
Little Rock, AR 72221

info@siblingrivalrypress.com

www.siblingrivalrypress.com

ISBN: 978-1-943977-43-7

Library of Congress Control No. 2017952252

This title is housed permanently in the Rare Books and Special
Collections Vault of the Library of Congress.

First Sibling Rivalry Press Edition, November 2017

SUBJECT TO CHANGE
TRANS POETRY & CONVERSATION

JOSHUA JENNIFER ESPINOZA
CHRISTOPHER SOTO
BEYZA OZER
CAMERON AWKWARD-RICH
KAY ULANDAY BARRETT

edited by
H. MELT

Dedicated to every trans, gender nonconforming, and queer person.
You are important, you matter, and you deserve more than just survival—
you deserve a world that recognizes your beauty and allows you to thrive.

EDITOR'S NOTE

"Subject to Change" was a monthly queer dance party in Chicago from 2011 to 2013. It was held at the Burlington and later Township, two bars located in Logan Square. Each night featured a different theme and a rotating roster of DJs, performance artists, and community organizations that benefited from the party. I found its intentions of supporting grassroots organizations and local artists admirable.

The dance party was organized by a collective of queer and trans people. Like most queer parties, it only lasted a few years. The name of the party has stuck with me—like many names of queer spaces that no longer exist. Naming is such an integral part of queer and trans communities. Queerness is always subject to change and trans people are, too. We all are.

Subject to Change is an anthology that I've dreamt of ever since I read *Troubling the Line: Trans & Genderqueer Poetry & Poetics*, which was edited by Trace Peterson and TC Tolbert. Before the publication of that book in 2013, I had not thought of myself as a "trans poet." I had not thought to put those two words and seemingly separate parts of myself together. I am forever indebted to *Troubling the Line* for creating space for me to exist as a trans poet. Reading the collection motivated me to continue the important work of celebrating trans poetry. I hope that *Subject to Change* inspires other trans poets to create spaces for their own work to live in the world.

Subject to Change features five poets who are unapologetically trans. I approached Sibling Rivalry Press about publishing this anthology because they released *Prime: Poetry & Conversation*, a groundbreaking and often overlooked anthology featuring five Black Queer poets: Darrel Alejandro Holnes, Saeed Jones, Rickey Laurentiis, Phillip B. Williams, and L. Lamar Wilson, along with an introduction by Jericho Brown. *Subject to Change* incorporates elements of the structure of *Prime* and features both poetry and interviews.

Joshua Jennifer Espinoza, Christopher Soto, beyza ozer, Cameron Awkward-Rich, and Kay Ulanday Barrett are all poets whose work makes me proud to be trans. Their work expresses the wide spectrum of trans experiences. I am honored to be able to share their work and do so in the hopes that more people begin to listen to trans people telling their own stories. It's time to listen to us.

– H. Melt

JOSHUA JENNIFER ESPINOZA

POEM (LET US LIVE)

I'm tired of abstraction.
No one says what they mean
and people die from it.
Where did this world come from?
Not nowhere.
Not nothing.
The dead trans women
you glance over
for a few seconds on Facebook
while deciding if the story is worth sharing
all came from somewhere.
Their bodies are not flowers
for you to whisper
to people you'll never know.
There were words that did this.
There were hands
and guns
and teeth
and flesh
and hair
and blood
and men
and women
and laws
and policies
and police
and witnesses
that did this.
How long can I keep tricking you
into thinking what I'm doing
is poetry
and not me begging you
to let us live?

A GUIDE TO READING TRANS LITERATURE

We're dying and we're really sad.
We keep dying because trans women
are supposed to die.
This is sad.

I don't have the words for my body
so I'll say I'm a cloud
or a mountain
or something pretty that people enjoy
so if I die
people will be like "Oh, that's sad."

Be sad about that.
It's okay to be sad.
It is sad when people die.
It is sad when people want to die.

I sometimes want to die but I don't!
I'm one of the lucky ones.
You can feel happy about that.
It's okay to feel happy about that.

Now pretend this is very serious:

History doesn't exist.
My body doesn't exist.
There's nothing left for you to be complicit in.

It's okay for you to feel happy about that.

Now pretend I am crying
right in front of you,
opening that wound up just for you.

Now pretend you can feel my pain.

Now pretend something in you
has been moved, has been transformed.

Now pretend you are absolved.

I DREAM OF HORSES EATING COPS

I dream of horses eating cops
I have so much hope for the future

or no I don't

Who knows the sound a head makes when it is asleep
My dad was a demon but so was the white man in uniform
who harassed him for the crime of being brown

There are demons everywhere
dad said
and he was right but not in the way he meant it

The sky over San Bernardino was a brilliant blue when the winds kicked in
All the fences and trash cans and smog scattered themselves
and the mountains were on fire every day

I couldn't wait to die or be killed
my woman body trapped in a dream

I couldn't wait to wake up
and ride off into the sunset
but there isn't much that's new anywhere

The same violence swallows itself and produces bodies
and names for bodies

I name my body girl of my dreams
I name my body proximity
I name my body full of hope despite everything
I name my body dead girl who hasn't died yet

I hope I come back as an elephant
I hope we all come back as animals
and eat our fill

I hope everyone gets everything they deserve

I IMAGINE ALL MY CIS FRIENDS LAUGHING AT TRANNY JOKES

I imagine all my cis friends laughing at tranny jokes
whenever I'm not around. I can hear the sound of rain
outside and I'm grasping for the words to say this. There
is nothing I love more than an honest storm. Broken dishes.
Dead grass. The time has come for me to be alive
and for you to stop speaking. Please stop speaking. Please, oh
please stop speaking. I have never felt as alone as this,
I say every day. I have never felt so alone. I've built houses
in corners of houses and filled them with all of my
longings. My strength. My pride. My beauty. My woman
self. I read another comments section of an article
about trans women and I want to die. To not exist. To let
them win. I don't let them win. I circle the drain
and kiss my fingers hello. I welcome them back. This complex
trauma responds only to the dialectical. Only to the heat
and the cool, the death and the life. Only then is it lifted
for a moment to let me breathe. I breathe the sweet air
and stare at the hillside, and then at the road, and then
at the cars, and then at the sky. All so unsure of themselves.
All so softly shaking in place. All so beautifully living.

EVERY MORNING I WALK THROUGH A FIELD

Every morning I walk through a field in my head
and I pick the weeds, water the flowers, scatter seeds,

set the trash heap on fire. I never speak a word—never
once do I have to hear the sound of my own voice, and

it is heaven, the blessing of erasure, the harmless
ego death extending far into the woods I dare not

explore. I am a light in the form of a girl, my strong
hands caressing my weak arms. I am my own warm

bath at the end of the day. I come home to myself
and practice breathing. It does not always go so

well and there are times I'd rather be the sky, be
the clouds, be the end of the storm dissipating

over open waters. This unique trans loneliness eats away
at me. It is always at hand, always coming, always

hungry for more of me. No one asks how they can
help and it's fine. I have my flowers. I have my

heap. I have the parts of my body that still belong
to me. I have the will to keep moving.

IN CONVERSATION WITH
JOSHUA JENNIFER ESPINOZA

First off, I honestly want to ask how you are doing in this moment, since the election of trump as the president of this country. What have you been thinking and feeling? How has this presidency affected you and people you know?

I'm scared, and everyone I know is scared, but the thing is—we were already scared before the election. trump has begun moving the evils of white supremacy, capitalism, borders, and prisons towards their logical conclusions. In other words, all of this was happening already. People who immigrated here were being deported. Black people were being murdered by police and imprisoned en masse. Indigenous people were having their land stolen and desecrated and were faced with violence for daring to resist. Queer and trans and gender nonconforming people were being abused and killed. trump shows us that the project of the U.S. was, in fact, always centered around oppression and terrorism against marginalized people.

I want to talk about your relationship to trans literature. In "A Guide to Reading Trans Literature," you write, "Now pretend something in you / has been moved, has been transformed. // Now pretend you are absolved." Why do you think people read trans lit—what are its limits and its possibilities? Do you see yourself in a lineage of trans writers, and are there any trans books that are particularly important to you?

I no longer believe there is such a thing as "trans lit." There are trans people who write, there are institutions that canonize certain writers as "trans lit," but I don't see trans lit as a stable or coherent genre. I also don't think it should be—it's important to look at who gets left out of conversations around trans lit. "Trans" as a concept is steeped in whiteness and colonial notions of what gender is. There are writers who identify as non-binary and/or gender nonconforming who don't have access to "capital-T" Transness in the same way that white trans people do. I want people to read and hear trans and gender nonconforming writers. I want us to be listened to and appreciated and loved. I want writers like Jayy Dodd, Venus Selenite, and Manuel Arturo Abreu to be listened to and appreciated and loved. I see myself in a lineage of writers who seek not to create a canon of trans lit but to question and resist its boundaries.

Those lines also seem directed at a cis audience. Do you think there is a difference between writing or performing for a cis versus a trans audience? Is that something you think about as a writer? Who is your ideal audience?

There's definitely a difference in how vulnerable I'm willing to let myself be, and how I'm able to use my vulnerability to a certain effect based on the audience. When performing, I'm more guarded around audiences primarily composed of cis white people, but I use these moments to challenge myself to make space for my body and my voice, and that can often be empowering, especially when audiences are receptive, sensitive, and willing to hear me.

In "Poem (Let Us Live)" you point out that there are laws, policies, and police that are killing trans women. This naming is so important, because it does not blame trans women for the violence they experience, as the media (in the rare cases they pay attention) often does in their reportage. "I Dream of Horses Eating Cops" is another poem where you discuss police brutality. Do you consider yourself a police abolitionist? Can you talk more about your thoughts on policing and the ways that the legal system impacts trans people?

I am a police and prison and border abolitionist. I'm against any system whose sole purpose is to abuse, exploit, and murder marginalized people in order to serve the interests of white capitalists. Poetry will not save the day, but as you said, naming these things can be a step towards resisting them.

So much of your writing is about existence and survival. You end "Poem (Let Us Live)" by asking, "How long can I keep tricking you / into thinking what I'm doing / is poetry / and not me begging you / to let us live?" Do you consider poetry as a tool for your survival? What helps you survive and validates your existence?

Writing poetry is just about the only way I know how to survive. It serves as both a way to name and unearth the unnamed and hidden realities of this world and as a tool for imagining new and better worlds. That sounds trite, but this naming and imagining truly does keep me alive.

One of the elements of your work that I love is your unique use of tone. There is a critical use of flippancy in your writing—you often shift between a mix of emotions, including sarcasm and sadness. Is this something you consciously developed as part of the voice in your writing? What purpose does this serve?

I think it's one part defense mechanism and one part an attempt to introduce some levity into deeply sad poems. It's also a survival tool—I couldn't really carry on with this work, with this life, unless I found a way to be humorous, sardonic, etc.

In "I Imagine All My Cis Friends Laughing at Tranny Jokes" you demand cis people to stop speaking. If there is one thing you could tell cis people, what would it be?

I would tell specifically *white* cis people to think critically about their own experiences of gender, to not take for granted the fact that gender is a system of control, of regulation, of power, of fear, and of shame. Investigating your own gender—whether you are cis or trans or anything else—allows you to experience the world in a new way, allows you to be more sensitive to the oppression faced by those whose gender is not legible within this system.

CHRISTOPHER SOTO

[SOMEWHERE IN LOS ANGELES] THIS POEM IS NEEDED

She charges her ankle bracelet // from the kitchen chair
       & Sunflowers in the white wallpaper [begin to wilt].

I wilt with them // before my sister // & her probation
       Officer [who comes over to the house unannounced].

Just as we are // preparing dinner // & what are we supposed to
       Do now. Cook for him?! Invite him to eat with us??

//

I am hacking the heads [from broccoli stems] & pretending
       His body is spread across the cutting board. [Ugh].

This officer keeps talking nonsense & nudging his eyes around
       The apartment. Looking for—drugs, alcohol,

Alchemy. My sister waits for him to leave & then begins to rant.
       Ramble about // her childhood // & how she used to be

[Before house arrest]. The confines of these plastered walls
       & Her monitored route to work // where

Every corner has a cop [coddling a liquor store]. Protecting their
       Notion of *freedom.* // My neighborhood eats fear.

//

Mothers are being // handcuffed & harassed. Homes are being
Crushed [like cigarette butts]. Everyone I know

Hates the racist police & wants a revolution. // But we seldom
Aim the gun... Have you heard // how the bullets

Sing their anthem // throughout the body?? // It sounds like
God shutting the door— Bang. Bang.

//

When it's dinnertime in heaven [& your officer's knocking]
Ignore him sister— let the door bruise.

[Let the bears devour our enemies]. We have no obligation
To open // ourselves // for those who do us harm.

ALL THE DEAD BOYS LOOK LIKE ME
for Orlando

Last time I saw myself die is when police killed Jessie Hernandez,

      A 17-year-old brown queer, who was sleeping in their car.

Yesterday, I saw myself die again. Fifty times I died in Orlando. And

      I remember reading Dr. José Esteban Muñoz before he passed.

I was studying at NYU, where he was teaching, where he wrote shit

      That made me feel like a queer brown survival was possible. But he didn't

Survive and now, on the dancefloor, in the restroom, on the news, in my chest

      There are another fifty bodies, that look like mine, and are

Dead. And I have been marching for Black Lives and talking about the police brutality

      Against Native communities too, for years now, but this morning

I feel it, I really feel it again. How can we imagine ourselves // We being black native

      Today, Brown people // How can we imagine ourselves

When All the Dead Boys Look Like Us? Once, I asked my nephew where he wanted

      To go to College. What career he would like, as if

The whole world was his for the choosing. Once, he answered me without fearing

      Tombstones or cages or the hands from a father. The hands of my lover

Yesterday praised my whole body. Made the angels from my lips, Ave Maria

      Full of Grace. He propped me up like the roof of a cathedral in NYC

Before we opened the news and read. And read about people who think two brown queers

      Cannot build cathedrals, only cemeteries. And each time we kiss

A funeral plot opens. In the bedroom, I accept his kiss, and I lose my reflection.

      I am tired of writing this poem, but I want to say one last word about

Yesterday, my father called. I heard him cry for only the second time in my life.

      He sounded like he loved me. It's something I am rarely able to hear.

And I hope, if anything, his sound is what my body remembers first.

IN SUPPORT OF VIOLENCE

Two-hundred Indian women killed their rapist on the courtroom floor of Nagpur in 2004.
When police tried to arrest lead perpetrators // the women responded "arrest us all."

//

In this windowless room // where he poured acid & stole money // arrest us all
In this windowless room [shut like the gut of an ox] arrest us all

Gored & gorge are words to describe a wound   Gorgeous // the opening
Of a blade inside his chest   *Gorgeous* // black galaxies, growing

                    Across his skin, we threw rocks & chili pepper
Arrest us all

On the railroad tracks // where he murdered our sisters & left their dead bodies
On the railroad tracks // where black ants began // biting crowns into

Calves //   The world is spinning and we're // falling from its bed
How could we mourn?   He kept killing // & threatening // & raping us

Arrest us all   On the red puddle // on the white courthouse floor
Arrest us all   We sawed his penis off // & tore his house // to rubble

  Look // the streets are swarming // in protests   [welcome home]
            The night is neon & buzzing like bumblebees

We never wanted to kill // only to stay alive // &
We waited like virgins // for the gentleness of strangers // to help or empathize.

SELF-PORTRAIT AS SONORAN DESERT

She walks across my chest—

                        dragging her shadow & fraying
                                [All the edges].

My nipples bloom // into cacti—

                   Fruit & flower.

She eats // then I do.

        —A needle pricks her.

I have only seen this woman // cry once—

                              Squeezed // like a raincloud.

She cried because // two white men.

[Two white men]

                Built a detention center—

                      From bone & clay.

[The first bone— my clavicle].   The second— her spine.

She howls

                      [As the fence // surrounds her].

She coughs &

Combs // the floor // my chest

                  [Shiv-shivering].

Inside the detention center—

               [She is named]   "immigrant" "illegal."

                     She loses 15 pounds &

Mental health & her feet are—

              Cracked tiles // dirty dishes.

This border—   is not a stitch [where nations meet].

This border is a wound //   where nations part.

HOME [CHAOS THEORY]

Home isn't merely a physical space
But also a philosophical one—

Often defined by a feeling of security.

Here, it's possible to [own] property
& feel completely homeless.

Here, it's possible to be sleeping on a park bench
& know you are home.

The last time I ran away

[To San Francisco]

There was this police officer hassling

A "homeless" woman

By the Powell Street Station.

The officer was telling her to move

Move

[Move on].

& the "homeless" woman responded

"Where? I have nowhere else to go!"

& the officer was telling her to

MOVE!!

[Move on].

But what he meant to say is

"You are too poor & brown to be in this neighborhood."

[When will we stop defining people
In terms of property ownership]?

[This is about the criminalization of poverty].

& the "homeless" woman responded
[To the officer]

"THIS IS MY HOME!!

I HAVE LIVED HERE FOR OVER TWENTY YEARS.
I WILL NOT MOVE!!!"

...
...

& the tourists watched

[As the police walked towards her].
[As the police went to grab her].
[As she continued yelling].

"I HAVE AIDS, I HAVE NO MONEY, I HAVE NOTHING LEFT.
     WHAT DO YOU WANT

FROM ME?! I'M GOING TO DIE HERE. JUST LEAVE ME ALONE
     & LET ME DIE!!!!"

. . .

. . .

              & the manner by which
              The "homeless" population
              Is [often] described is
              Extremely othering.

. . .

. . .

I've heard some of my closest comrades
Speak of the "homeless" population

[In grand generalizations] such as

                  "I don't care
                  If homeless people
                  Spend my money
                  On drugs or alcohol."

As if "homelessness" were a singular portrait
                [A singular experience].

As if I had never been homeless.
[As if I were not sitting // directly beside them].

& it is hard for me
To imagine these comrades
Making such generalizations
& assertions about any other
Population [of people].

Consider the statements—

"I don't care if black people spend government
money on drugs or alcohol."
"I don't care if native people spend government
money on drugs or alcohol."

It's a strange
Place to be
When your
Friends start sounding
Like racists
In the Democratic
Party. [When you
Remember
Such ignorance
Still exists].

& somewhere
There is a book
I want to write
Called "Anarchist
Island." Somewhere
There is a zine
I want to write
Called "Gay Daddy
Loves
Cum Dumpster."

[Gay Daddy & Cum Dumpster
Are alter-egos I created after
Rory died].

Never mind...

Let's talk about the ownership of
Land as a colonial construct
& how the police state was created
To protect stolen property.

Or

Let's talk about queer pessimism
& how to decentralize happiness //
[How we can still create lives of
contentedness & meaning].

Or

Let's talk about the night Rory crashed his car
Into the center divider of the 405 Freeway.

[We were so high]

With our hands like kites

Outside the window.

Music blaring.

Tonsils clapping

In laughter!

. . . .

. . . .

When Rory crashed his car

       The metal dented, airbags deployed
       Smoke smoked.

Windows broke
    [Into granulates of glass].

        The cops laid flares

[Or broken hearts]
     Along the concrete floor.

& TRAFFIC STOPPED FOR US.

For us.

       We walked across // the paisley freeway

[Hiding a plastic baggie
Of mushrooms].

    We called our fathers

     For a ride home.

Rory went to his address

        & I went to mine.

My father & I

     Didn't talk on the drive back.

[The space between us was a walrus

With sharp tusks].

& the home // my father brought me to

Was a million pomegranate seeds

Waiting to explode.

...

...

Rory [later] told me about the argument that
He had with his father.

[Such is expected].

& when Rory crashed his car.

& when Rory crashed his car.

& when Rory crashed his car.

& when Rory crashed his car.

& when Rory crashed his car.

& when Rory crashed his car.

[Too much changed].

...

We used to sneak out & sleep in the backseat
Of that car // every night that

My father would
Whoop my ass.

[So almost every night]
We'd sleep there.

Rory drove a green Subaru Outback

Which became my "home."
My "refuge." //
My "safe-place." //

& when his car hit the center divider

Then...

I never considered myself to be
that kind of "homeless"

[Like the woman in San Francisco
With the rotting hands].

BUT sometimes

[When] my father would

Press me beneath
[The moon's bottom lip].

& I had nowhere else to go.

& I had to leave his house.

& I could no longer stay with Rory.

& I was too afraid to call other friends // or family members.

&

SOMETIMES

When the church was closed.

& the park was being patrolled.

& I got tired of just walking around.

& I would hum songs to myself.

[The love songs of extinct birds].

& those days // I could never create ART.

[Just these shitty narrative poems].

[Just tangential thoughts, escapes, attempts]

Trying NOT to tell you—

Yes.

[I have been that kind of "homeless" before].

When the moon was
A broken headlight
& each star hung
Imprisoned by its sky.

[I was that kind of "homeless"].

I used to sleep in the prairies
Behind the fire station.
There was this old abandoned oak

Tree, with a tire swing.
& I made walls out of
Recycled tarp [I strung
From its branches]. & I stole
Plastic chairs from
The nearby housing tracks.
Then I dug & I flattened
& I swept the dirt floor
Where I laid my sleeping bag
[On top of the cardboard tiles].

There are twenty poems I want to write for you—

About tattered socks & cheap tattoos.

About dumpster diving for food.

[All the boys I kissed for a bed to sleep in].
All the boys I wanted to be with

To bring "home"

[But couldn't].

IN CONVERSATION WITH
CHRISTOPHER SOTO

Your chapbook *Sad Girl Poems* was published by Sibling Rivalry Press. How did the book find a home there? What has your experience been like working with the press?

There were only three presses that I was really interested in for my chapbook: Sibling Rivalry Press, YesYes Books, and Organic Weapon Arts. I remember thinking, "If none of these presses accept my work then I'll just print it as a DIY zine and give it to friends myself." I'm not too good at being patient about poetry publishing or waiting for acceptance. Now, after having gone through the publishing process with my chap and other poems, I think I'll be a bit more patient and open-minded with my first full length, hopefully.

I wanted to be with Sibling Rivalry Press because that's where Ocean Vuong and Saeed Jones got their start. I respect a lot of poets on that press. I'm grateful for all the work that Bryan and Seth have put into making my chapbook. They have been such sweethearts and so supportive of my work throughout this process.

You're going on a tour to end queer youth homelessness at the same time as the release of your chapbook. Why did you decide to focus on queer youth homelessness, and how will the tour work to end it?

I talk a bit about queer youth homelessness in my chapbook, so it seemed like a logical connection. I think it's an under-spoken, under-addressed reality within the queer community, which impacts so many people. According to the Williams Institute at UCLA, about 40% of homeless youth are LGBT. I wanted to better understand myself in relation to queer youth homelessness and the state of queer youth homelessness in general. By talking about queer youth homelessness,

I'm also able to address a host of other issues which are important to me, such as domestic violence, police brutality, the decriminalization of sex work and drug usage, and the failures of marriage equality and gay assimilation.

Pertaining to ending queer youth homelessness, I'm not sure that it can be accomplished by one chapbook tour. I view this as more of a consciousness-raising effort; an attempt at creating community dialogue. Consciousness raising is important, but it is hard to track the direct impact of consciousness raising on a community. If possible, I would also like to help raise funds and provide direct services, too, but I have to realize my limitations on this tour. I can't be every department in a non-profit organization.

One white person just wrote me the other day saying my work was "unhelpful," and in my head I'm thinking, "Why don't you organize your own fucking tour and launch your own campaign instead of lazily criticizing mine?" It takes a lot for queer and trans people of color to have enough confidence to speak publicly in a world where our lives and work are so constantly devalued or seemingly non-existent. It infuriates me when cis, white people think they have a right to speak to me that way. MEDIOCRE BITCHES WILL NEVER SILENCE ME.

In your chapbook, you talk a lot about home. You say, "Home isn't merely a physical space" and is "often defined by a feeling of security." Where are some places that you feel home? Do you ever feel that people can provide a sense of home?

Right now, New York is starting to feel like home. Some of my friends and family feel like home. I don't have home in a physical property. I'm not sure that I ever did. I would like to create a physical home in New York, but it is so expensive, and I have moved every year since I've been here. Always changing neighborhoods, always changing roommates. And yes, I think that people can be a sort of home. My mother feels like home.

In your poem "Ars Poetica" you write, "This is such a useless fucking poem." Your next poem starts off "I hate these poems." This made me wonder, do you feel there are limits to poetry and what it can do? If so, what are they?

Good observation. This chapbook was a pain for me to write. Brenda Shaughnessy once said to me, "You seem like you're frustrated with what you're writing." I was in her workshop with Javier Zamora, Monica Sok, and Jameson Fitzpatrick (who all write such crafted and intentional and linear poems). I felt too messy and illogical, like my poems lacked craft and voice and perspective and form and lyric. I was discovering my voice in this chapbook and pushing too much to be like other poets around me. I was tired of writing over and over and over again the same poems about daddy problems and being traumatized. I wanted to create something new and was unable to do so.

In my personal opinion, this chapbook functions in a very similar manner to a first book for many other poets. It is very close to the adolescent "I," and it is exploring closed forms such as the villanelle and trying to flex poetic muscles. It also steals very much from the poets I read. At first, I hated these poems. Now I am more appreciative of them as part of my growing process and learning process as a poet.

My new work, the voice that I have come to recognize as my own (which not many folks have read), shifts away from the personal narrative and is more directly concerned with the political. My new work tries to find the high lyric in relationship to punk (as Lorca did with gypsy music, as Langston did with blues). My frustrations with *Sad Girl Poems* were not with the limitations of poetry as a vehicle for political action. My frustrations with *Sad Girl Poems* were as an individual writer who was losing and rediscovering a poetic voice.

You're the editor of *Nepantla: A Journal Dedicated to Queer Poets of Color* and were also part of the Undocupoets Campaign. What impact do you think these projects have on the literary world, and what do you think is the relationship between poetry and activism?

I'm not sure what the impact is. What metrics are we using to calculate impact? For me, the impact is really only visible when I get messages from other people, like I did this morning (from another poet who is starting a journal dedicated to queer indigenous writers, called *Cloudthroat*) citing *Nepantla* as an inspiration. That's when I feel the impact. Otherwise, I often don't feel the reach of my little poems or interviews or projects. Maybe I'm too close to its center.

And the relationship between poetry and activism is long and complicated to discuss. It has looked so different for different poets in different locations over time. I trace my lineages to June Jordan in the U.S., I trace my lineages to Roque Dalton in El Salvador. I understand that political poetry has cost some people their lives and safety. I am thinking about poets such as Ashraf Fayadh, who was given a death sentence by the Saudi Arabian government for his words. I'm not sure what impact my work has, but I understand that activism has repercussions. I understand that silence has repercussions, too.

You've written about being gender nonconforming, and I was wondering if you could mention some GNC people who inspire you and/or affirm your existence?

Alok and Janani from DarkMatter are close friends of mine, and their work constantly inspires me. Also, Joshua Allen is an activist and prison abolitionist based out of NYC whom I love dearly and find strength in. Other gender nonconforming activists and artists of color in New York City who inspire me are Jamal Lewis and Kiki Williams. I have been a bit of a recluse lately, mainly talking to my partner, other poets, and my poems. But the existence and vision and voices of these people give me strength.

The introduction to your chapbook includes your vision of a dream poetry world where there is more support for POC poets and publishers, along with the call for poets to get paid for their work. What would your dream world outside of a poetry context be like?

Put minimally, in my dream world everyone would have access to food, safety, and shelter. I don't think this is too much to ask. I think my political framework is actually very deeply rooted to my relationship with Catholicism. I grew up Catholic. I always thought Jesus was extremely radical and political. He was born homeless, hung out with sex workers, was an anti-capitalist, and was crucified by the state. I think my dream world is very parallel with some Catholic ideologies. I believe in the redistribution of resources and helping those who are in need of help.

BEYZA OZER

A PHONE CALL BETWEEN ME & ALLAH

It is hard to open windows when people are always screaming & I can
be better.

↬

Technically I could start over, but I'd rather be alone when I change.

↬

There isn't a word in Turkish that explains my gender
but I know you knew what I meant when I said what I said.

↬

A woman wearing a headscarf is holding a sign reading *please help me*,
mashallah
& I have never felt farther away from you.

↬

Allahu Akbar
Allahu Akbar
Allahu Akbar
Allahu Akbar

I STILL HAVE VERY OLD HANDS & HERE IS THAT LETTER I PROMISED

here is an idea: you are living on earth with me.

here is another idea: we are not alone

& never have been/never will be.

this is a poem in which two things will happen/are happening:

you are thinking about how the way waves

move makes you think of a certain sound

while i am remembering the time i thought

my grandmother was dead when she really

just fell asleep awkwardly on the couch.

please don't laugh at me. please know

that the last time i saw my grandfather

was probably the last time

i saw my grandfather. let me move along.

we are living on earth together. here is an idea:

this is not the only place in the milky way we have been.

i came from the star SMSS J031300.362670839.3

which is 6,000 light-years away from earth

to live here with you. i hope that is good enough.

so, we are here living on earth together,

specifically in north america, specifically in the united states,

specifically in illinois, specifically in chicago. here is another idea:

we are here in chicago & you are kissing me on

a mountain of hard snow, mostly ice,

& there is a dead rabbit hanging off the

edge of our mountain. i look for the right

stick to push it off into lake michigan

so it can have a softer place to rest.

my arms are too short. here is an idea:
you are two inches taller than me so you
try to push the rabbit off our mountain,
but as soon as you feel its flesh through the
vibrations of the right stick you jolt.
you are crying & we leave the rabbit
alone so it can say goodbye to the ground
& fall into the lake naturally after the snow/ice
has melted. until then, we climb up the side
of a lifeguard chair to create our own level between
the lake & the troposphere.
here is a story because i love you:
when i told an entire room i wanted to
kill myself, mom got a phone call.
mom called me after she got the call & cried at work
with all the windows open. mom asked if i was ok.
mom said, *do you need to see anyone?*
i might need to see someone. mom wasn't home
one day after i got back from work. dad said mom
called the mental hospital & checked herself in.
dad followed me with a box of tissues after i ran out
of the house without shoes on. dad called mom
when i got home from crying at the park & gave me
the phone but i am a child & if i had shoes on at that
moment, they would be untied. mom said it wasn't my fault.
mom, i said, *it is.* mom cried & i didn't call her again.
dad picked mom up four days later. kenan asked mom about the hospital
& i said i had to use the bathroom & threw up in the shower.
i could only hear one sound out of thousands

playing in the background. i haven't spoken to my mom
about that summer since the length of a river ago.
but this is what it taught me: every ghost has a
future. the ghosts are screaming at me, *FAIL BETTER*.
here is a fact to change the subject:
my grandmother taught me the word no
& the word fuck, in that order. this was before
i thought she had died on the couch with her mouth
wide open. my grandmother is a cluster of stars
that hasn't been discovered yet. my mom gets upset
when i cut my hair shorter than my brother's
but she reminds me of the most tired supernova.
here is what i would tell my grandfather
if i could translate it into turkish: *hearing your voice*
makes my bones ungrow. here is what i would
tell my mom if i wasn't so scared: *i want to visit a room*
full of rollercoasters with you. here is what
i want my grandmother to know before she leaves me:
i'm sorry, but i am getting your favorite flower tattooed on my skin.
anyway, askim, canim, sevgilim, whatever you prefer,
this is a poem for you. why do pigeons stay with us
even though we treat them so badly? you were there with
me when i got an outline of one tattooed on my
inner arm & i wish i was lying when i said it didn't hurt
but it really didn't & that scares me. sometimes i am flying
& other times i am swimming through thick air.
here's a question: how would you feel if instead of our skin
we had that cloth your favorite stuffed animal
was made out of growing up? it wouldn't feel as

breakable or lonely but there are two things
i want to tell you: one is that we should try to
build a waterfall from scratch & the other
involves us jumping off of it holding hands.
we could take an umbrella with us to soften our
fall like that episode of gilmore girls where logan took rory
to the life and death brigade event, though we probably wouldn't need it
because our new skin would make us feel safe like we did
back in 1996. it is not easy to love. i hope saying this
doesn't cross any boundaries but i made you those boundaries
& don't worry because i will never take them away from you
even if you ask me to leave your birthday party.
here is a word: celestial. here is its meaning:
that time at the beach when each wave met
with the shore & disappeared into something
bigger than us. here is a fact: you were meant for the sea
& if anything in this life is fair you will find a good home.
i just wanted to remind you that manners don't mean anything
& if a man asks you to smile it's okay to tell him to fuck off.
i will take you back to the beach one day & i might even wear a
bathing suit, but probably not. the feeling of sand between my
toes still makes me feel dirty, but i'm starting to enjoy podcasts more.
here is what i've been wanting to ask you all day: do you think
the L tracks will always be there? they've been up for so
long & all we can do is complain about how loud they are
or how long it takes us to get to work. but what i really
want to ask you is how many times have you seen someone
give money to a person asking for it & how did it make you feel?
one time i was on the bus going home & i saw a woman sitting

on the corner of state & madison with a sign that said
IF YOU CAN HELP ME YOU ARE BEAUTIFUL & IF YOU CANNOT
YOU ARE STILL BEAUTIFUL, MASHALLAH & i got off the bus
even though the next one wouldn't come for another 20 minutes but
i needed to look at her & say mashallah so i did & gave her the
five dollars i had left in my pocket. i said mashallah & she looked at me
like i wasn't scared or alone or fucked or sad even though
i am all of those things & said you are beautiful & kissed my hand while
10,000 buses passed us by. this is when i started to cry & decided to walk
to michigan & delaware & the wind was so sharp it cut my face
so when i got on the bus there were scratches where my smooth skin
used to be & my tears made them sting, but i felt beautiful so i didn't care.
i haven't seen her since but here is an idea: we'll make each other bracelets
& yours will say i'd rather be drinking wine & mine will say gender is a social construct
& after you leave to go to your apartment i will make a t-shirt that says
i am so happy i never killed myself & my mom never did either & she is a great mom. here
is an apology: i'm sorry if i don't say i love you enough in this poem & i'm sorry
because i don't know how to say it in real life & poetry is the dreamiest way
to write something down. what i'm saying is, yes, i will dance with you
the next time you ask me. what i'm saying is, van gogh painted with
blues but i don't think he knew what blue ever meant. people have always
told me that i should read more about van gogh & his life & that i might be able
to relate to it or him somehow & i tell people that i know three things:
one is that if there is a constant noise in space it might sound like the way you
brush your hair. another is that we were always supposed to be moons.
the last is that we know nothing about what goes on underwater
& that is fucking terrifying, but i love you anyway.
this poem is definitely for you, i want you to know that & i want you to
know that it's also for your grandma jones. i know how much she loves you

even though i never met her but i've seen the ocean at least once
& your eyes over a million times & she is in both places so technically
we have met before. here is an idea: if you ever go bald or i ever lose
my sight i can kiss hair back onto your head & you can kiss cones
back into my eyes, deal? deal. meanwhile, let's eat clouds for breakfast
or wait until the rain holds up. let's google what it would feel like
to swallow a star whole. i think it would feel like kissing you on a bunk bed
or a pile of french toast or a bathtub filled with dogs. here is an idea: i'm here
loving you always. here is an idea: me screaming *this is what a sad person in love
looks like* into my invisible megaphone & yes, i still have it saved from last time,
the paint is just chipping off a little. don't get me wrong, i am a sad person but
there is a difference between being sad & being alive & before, i didn't feel alive.
i have come so far & cried in so many buses to get to you. here is an idea:
you stay here with me for as long as you want & we go to the beach when it
isn't so cold that your toes turn purple. we listen to a wave & the shore
meet for the first time. here is the truth: you make me feel so 1999 & yes,
that was the year i tried on my dad's clothes & everything
hiding inside my skin felt like it was moving again.

WHEN I KISS YOU, A CASKET OPENS
after june 12, 2016

this is not terrorism
this is toxic masculinity
made in the USA
when my mother hears
about orlando
she doesn't look at me
the next day is three years
to the night we first kissed
& it actually meant something
to both of us
but i am imagining us
buried in the ground
because when a man looks at us
all i feel is sickness & anger
because when a man looks at us
i already know
what he is going to do
once, at the beach,
when we kissed in the water
& one of them asked us
to do it again
in exchange for brunch
once, holding hands
& crossing the street
when one of them yelled at us
looking down from a window
in a bar next to his girlfriend
once, when i was kissing you goodbye
in the rain & a group of them
asked to join in

i am so tired of being scared
i am so tired of seeing us die
i am so tired of ignoring your kiss
when we are outside
& surrounded by the things
that kill us every day
i am sure that my death
is going to happen
at the hand of someone else
& when it does happen
i will think about once
when i saw you laughing
when i was sad & honestly,
i just want my mom
to say something about this
but i know she won't
so i will just remember
the last time she laughed
something i rarely hear
& that will be the sound
my body will feel first

DREAMISH

Take a moment to imagine the
moon with arms. To imagine
something impossible.
This is where I tell you
to break it apart. Take the pieces
& place them in your pocket
for next time. Now, we are required
to surrender in this moment
of blush, this big fall upwards.
When the air around you clutches
its breath, it is because the air
is happy to see you. Here is the thing
about doors: there is always something
behind them. Here is the thing
about windows: you can always see
what's right in front of you. I want
to see the origins of silence. Of
a steering wheel. A glass house on fire.
The writing of these moments is never
done. We're all waiting for Lake Michigan
to do something amazing. There's never
a perfect time to be melted
& isn't that the point of it all?
To not know the next time
it will be appropriate to break down
in an airport miles away from home.
When we fall apart, the pages follow.
We work them into our skin, like a poem.

TO LEARN THE SPACE WE HOLD

To turn into a dark midnight.

To start a fire

in the home of your heart.   To understand

the nonexistent center of   the universe.

I gather my dreams, cycle

them through the blood   of the people I love.

They tell me I can build a flower without any   water

& I believe them,   so I do it. A mother

is magic, can make the unwanted mess disappear. A grandmother,

a constellation
that has yet to be discovered.

A father, working until his hair falls out.

An aunt,   glass made of tulip.

& A brother, who turns joy into fire & makes

the two combine into music.

When love can reach   the moon   if I   cannot.

When a cloth lullaby can welcome sleep. I know

some things   will not change.

IN CONVERSATION WITH
BEYZA OZER

There are many references to home in your work. You are currently based in Chicago and grew up here. There are references to Lake Michigan, I-94, and Washtenaw in your writing. You have family in Skokie, in Rogers Park, in Turkey. In the title poem of your book *Fail Better* you write, "I'm living in two different countries at the same time / both are war-torn / both scare white people." Where do you consider home? How have your homes affected your writing?

Home is difficult. Home has been assigned to me, and I've also chosen a lot of places I call home—with my friends, the people I love, in my bed watching *Buffy*. What I consider home is where I feel like a part of me stays when I leave it. This doesn't necessarily always have to be where I'm comfortable or happy. That's a common misconception of what home should be or mean to somebody, but I don't always think that's the case. Home is supposed to make you grow and learn, and I've done that with many people in many places, specifically in Chicago and in Turkey.

This process of learning what home means to me has influenced my writing by allowing me the chance to imagine what home would be if I could never go back to it. How would I feel if I could never go back to Istanbul again? Write it down. What would I do without the company of my grandmother? Write it down. Then, if and when any of my fears come true, at least I can remember a time that wasn't the case. Dual citizenship has its ups and downs, and I think not knowing where to be at any point in time can feel painful, like I'm disassociating. In Turkey, I want to go back to Chicago, and in Chicago, I feel like I should be in Turkey. Both places feel foreign, or like some part of me doesn't belong there. This can be said about a lot of aspects in my life: gender, sexuality, mental health. But I'm growing either way.

We work together at Women & Children First bookstore and the Poetry Foundation. These are spaces that have not always been welcoming to trans people, people of color, queer people—those outside the norms of feminism or poetry. As I mentioned at your book release, working with another trans person has been really important to me. Do you think it's important for trans writers to have relationships with each other? How can trans writers better support each other, and how can cis people better support trans writers and people as well?

I definitely think institutions founded years ago have a certain level of misunderstanding, no matter their initiatives to be "inclusive." This is true of both of those places, but feminism is always moving forward, mainstream or not, and I'm so proud of how far Women & Children First has come. I don't know where I would be without the first poetry book I bought from there (by another gender nonconforming writer, Andrea Gibson), or my first book of feminist theory. Of course, there are going to be issues of transphobia, queerphobia, Islamophobia everywhere, but having someone who relates with your identity at your workplace is vital.

Before these two jobs, I was working at restaurants or a shitty used bookstore where I was surrounded by men twice my age that would constantly make me uncomfortable or try to come onto me. That is such a toxic experience that I would never wish on anyone. When you're in that environment, you cannot do your work to its full potential, and it isn't fair for anyone to ask that of you. It's so fucking important for trans people to stick together. Without you or other trans folks in my life, I would feel ultimately alone. I have many cis friends I love and admire in my life, but they will never be able to know how I feel when a customer misgenders me and I have to just take it, or when my internship doesn't care about my health or emotions enough to create a space for me to use the bathroom.

By just listening to trans people and not thinking about transness in terms of their own identities, cis people can make the lives of trans people much easier. We would feel loved and like we matter, and that's all any human being wants. Until then, I will support trans writers who consider my identity valid, though I've met many who do not believe being non-binary is real. People should just learn to respect others, writers or not, but folks should respect and support writing that doesn't always relate to them or their experiences.

The opening poem of your book is called "A Phone Call Between Me & Allah." After Orlando, I remember you writing a Facebook post about being both queer and Muslim. You begin the poem "I've Watched Myself Die Twice This Week," with the line "41 times in Istanbul, 49 in Orlando." You often discuss the intersections between queer and Muslim identities. Can you talk more about how those intersections play out in your writing and in your life?

When I was in middle school, I was more afraid of coming out as Muslim than coming out as queer. I'm still not sure why. I feel like people can look at me and tell that I'm some kind of queer or trans, but my Muslim identity is a mystery to people, even after they learn my name or where I'm from. For example, the other night I was outside of a bar around the corner from my apartment in Lincoln Square. A man was talking to me, trying to get to know who I was, and asked me about my name. I told him I was from Turkey, then he began to tell a story about his bad experiences with Turkish folks, making the conversation come around back to him and his feelings. He then asked me why I don't wear a hijab. Like, what the fuck? Why would you ask somebody that? Not only have I been confused about my relationship to Islam and religion my entire life, but these last few years have been even harder in terms of gender and transness. I never considered wearing a hijab even before coming out as not-a-woman, because I thought my people and culture hated me for being queer. All of these intersections ultimately pull me apart and keep me strung together at the same time.

You are really obsessed with space. You wear a NASA sweatshirt a lot. You use the metaphors of space repeatedly throughout your writing. Another trans poet, Joshua Jennifer Espinoza, has a poem about the moon being trans. How does outer space relate

to trans people? Why do you think the concept of space is useful to trans writers?

Space is constantly shifting and expanding, and human beings are learning more and more about space every day. Space is never fixed, and that's the most beautiful thing. Space allows us to think outside of ourselves, our experiences, our lives, and focus on something bigger, more significant. When something is weighing down on me in my day-to-day life, I think about the words Carl Sagan shared with us, or scroll through NASA's Twitter feed. It makes me feel like I'm never alone, because we aren't. Someone came up with an equation called the Drake Equation specifically to find other life in space. I use writing poems about space to reach out to other people who feel the same way I do.

You write, "There isn't a word in Turkish that explains my gender." Throughout your book, the issue of communication, especially with your family, comes up frequently. How do you explain your gender? How do you communicate with people across barriers of language, culture, and identity?

My family knows little about my gender identity. I haven't been able to come up with a way to tell them how to address or support me. All I know is that my brother, a 16-year-old in high school, respects the pronouns of trans and gender nonconforming kids at his school without a second thought. It always makes me cry because I'm so proud of his character.

Explaining gender to people outside of my family hasn't been successful either, especially while talking to cis women, who I find myself around most often. These are coworkers, my peers, customers, other poets. Language barriers don't usually come into play here, and I don't think the idea of barriers between culture and linguistics should be an excuse for ignorance. Basically, this is a learning process that I haven't perfected, because I don't think it can be. Communicating with acts of love and kindness are universal. That's all I really know.

You are a constant critic of outdated modes of feminism. What do you think feminism needs at this moment in time to progress? What are some of the ways that feminism has failed you?

Feminism needs to put Muslim, Black, Queer, Brown, Disabled, Trans, and other marginalized voices at the front. Period. When we have those voices telling us how they feel, what they are going through in their lives, and how we can help them, then feminism is doing what it is supposed to do. That isn't happening now to its full potential, and that is the most basic thing society can do to ensure the safety of these people.

The idea and practice of feminism has failed me in many ways, but it has saved me, too. The feminists I looked up to when I was 15 are not the same feminists I look up to now because I have changed and become more inclusive as the years have gone by. Basic white feminism that introduces folks, especially young people, to the idea can be very heteronormative and hurtful to people who do not fit in any binary or societal norm. Thankfully, most people choose to learn from their mistakes. I have, and my brand of feminism supports the fact that we don't always get everything right on the first try. This isn't an excuse to be oblivious, though. In my opinion, the most essential parts of feminism are to be inclusive of all people and to use your privileges to back up marginalized voices when they need it, but not to overpower them. If we take those simple steps, we can only progress.

At the time of this interview, you are 21 years old. You have already accomplished so much as a writer—publishing a book, editing a journal, working for a poetry press. Where do you see yourself in five to ten years? Fifty years? How do you envision your future?

I feel like this is a question that I can't really answer right now. I'm at a time in my life where nothing is certain. I'm graduating college. I thought I had a job lined up and ready for me at a foundation that doesn't support or care about who I am or how I feel. Some very important people who have shaped me are getting ready to leave Chicago, which is a city I have trouble thinking about abandoning. Everything is very up in the air. All I know is that I want to keep art in my life for as long as I can because it gives me purpose. Art, activism, and hope keep me alive.

Right now, I'm waiting for my life to begin. That doesn't necessarily answer your question, and I owe you an answer that is satisfying and clear, but it doesn't exist. Nothing is for certain when you are trans or queer or living in a country that won't guarantee your rights because of your identity. I want the rest of my life to be dedicated to changing that. If I had it my way, I would get a full ride at some grad school that would pay me to teach and learn at the same time. I always want to be learning and showing what I absorb to other people, and if I could do that in an environment that I know will respect my work and who I am, then that's all I can really ask for.

In 50 years I want to have touched the moon at least once in my life. I have this recurring thought about what I want to happen after I die. I want whoever loves me the most, whoever is left in my family, to shoot my ashes into outer space. I looked it up; it's an actual thing. I should probably start saving for that.

CAMERON AWKWARD-RICH

STILL LIFE

to Lawrence Jackson, arrested in Chicago for wearing a dress, 1881

A figure in a room. Black dress slit
up the thigh, a voice issues from the seam.

I sit in the dark & watch your hips,
your practiced walk.

//

Somewhere, there is a photograph
of me in a strapless dress. Me, flexing

my grin, my skinny arms. An image
won't show you the fight

at its edges—my girlfriend shining
like a pearl, her father's finger

on the shutter, the compromise
beneath the skirt.

//

If I can see you only in the moment
you are caught, what kind of we

does that make? Rows of dark bodies
hunched against the page, above

the page. In the archive of ink
& yellow trees, there you are

before the judge, offering to leave
the city, to walk away with nothing

in your pockets. No pockets.
This, you think, is what they want

from you. To look & not see you
standing.

//

What happens after that?
The trail ends with you, framed

by dark. They don't want us to leave,
exactly. Instead, to not have to look

to know we're there. Anything
can be made into a cage—

garment, sentence, cage.

//

I draw a frame around the frame,
a bright afternoon in Indiana

on your shoulders, dress
black & spun in a field of gold,

dress a knot of brazen black
birds, the body not a question.

ESSAY ON THE THEORY OF MOTION

You remember reading a poem about a boy driving his grandmother to the library across town. Someone said that the car is a perfect device for giving a poem the feeling of motion, though you think the two must end up back at the grandmother's house eventually, must walk hallways lined with family ghosts, all smiling through the window of a photograph & is that *motion*, really? This tendency to cross & recross the small terms of our own lives?

//

They expect me to talk about Newton. Fine. An object at rest stays at rest. An object in motion stays in motion. Friction has many names — it's no surprise that when the train stops, so do you.

//

What else is true? You beg each thing to answer. You make mouths for the answer to crawl through. You bite the inside of your cheek. You paint the world red all the way through.

//

I'm only kidding. You can't expect everything to speak your language. To use these new mouths for what you imagine mouths are for. After all, you make a mouth on your upper thigh, the doctor calls it a wound, your dumb hands at work again. You can't get your body to tell the secret. Can't get it to tell you anything at all.

//

Anyway, you've begun to suspect that *theory* is less movement toward truth & more movement through a series of puns.

For example, a queer theorist—you don't know who, but imagine their white spectacled face floating above a soft butch sweater—once wrote that they feel most at home in airports, because there everyone is *in transition*.

//

(Let's get the obvious out of the way—you were a girl & then you weren't. You moved into a boy & the girl moved into misplaced language, into photographs.)

//

Get it? Gender is a country, a field of signifying roses you can walk through, or wear tucked behind your ear.

Eventually the flower wilts & you can pick another, or burn the field, or turn & run back across the tracks.

THE CHILD FORMERLY KNOWN AS _____

is what your father calls you now.   Yes, you know
your father loves you
            but each time he will not name you

                        you feel a hole
bang open.   Black pit.   Runs straight through you
      like a tunnel,
                  which is what it is.

There are tracks laid in the tunnel in you & a train.
                              Yes, that's right, a train
            & on the other end, a little girl.

      The train is where each thing made for her that happens in your life
goes to travel to her & sometimes
            you think you will die—

last night the man tugging at his crotch
            says *Have a good night girl* or maybe he doesn't
                  grab his crotch & means nothing or means well
      but what does it matter?
                  He boards the train
            with your father & your first girlfriend & the state of Michigan
                  & they all want to see the girl

& you're carrying a train full of people who want you gone
                        or think you are gone.

But then the train is full & leaves
                  its station & leaves the hole
                        engine warm & then
      it all feels   faintly ridiculous—

who does that man think you are, anyway?
Even if you are a girl, you don't look like the kind
who would want him, though you do
in another life where he says *girl* with a slightly different inflection
& means he is the kind of man who wants a boy to ruin him.
To carve a hole & move inside.

But that isn't how it happened.
You're the one with the hole

with the little girl inside the hole
with the father standing at the edge, calling & calling
for her & never you
& you can't blame him—

you'd rather be her
or at least bury her, seal her shut
or shut her up
& in the end, isn't that what we all want?

To not feel so
split?   To carry an image of ourselves
inside ourselves & know exactly what
we mean

when we say *I*— .   *I*—   .

I— ?

THEORY OF MOTION (3): ANOTHER MIDDLE-CLASS BLACK KID TRIES TO NAME IT

I used to dream about a woman trapped inside
a burning house. That isn't how she went—

my grandmother. Instead, her city moved
inside her like a drunk man's fist.

All I know about my father's mother are these holes
in her, the holes she left. My father, pulled over

to the side of the road, crying a song
through the radio. I think her grief moved

into my father when he was born & into his daughters
when we were born & I'm sure someone's tried

to tell you the blues is only music, *but the radio
the radio.*

//

Once, my teacher bought me a cheeseburger & asked
how come the other black kids weren't more like me.

Once, a girl pinned me to the wall until I called myself
(or her) *nigga* & all week I wore her fingers as a bruise.

Once, I watched my teacher tell that other brown girl
her language was too beautiful to belong to her.

Those years, I wore cargo shorts through the winter,
books in each pocket, little hallways full of words
that weren't our own.

//

Is there a word for a child talking to himself
or no one?   I've said *ghost*

but I do have skin & a father, after all. Hands
after all, dirt colored & not buried in the dirt.

Sure, I've been opened the way girls are opened.
Sure, I've gone missing in the dark.

Sure, I've looked at my sister & seen a woman
caught in flames. But we have pills for that.

We have money for pills for that.

//

Please—

what's the word for being born of sorrow
that isn't yours? For having a family?

For belonging nowhere? Not even
your body. Especially not there.

ESSAY ON THE AWKWARD / BLACK / OBJECT
after m awkward, my father

There are at least two theories about love.
Both begin as violence. The subject
encounters the object & a slit opens
inside him. Love at first sight. Harriet's
master sees her as if for the first time &
now must have her. She wakes in the
night to a terrible face rising above her,
a wasted moon. The question is: once
made into an object-for-the-other, how
can the thing-for-itself survive?

//

In the airport / the bar / the movie theatre
/ the grocery store someone looks at you,
your face, then your face in the plastic of
your card, then the card, then the card,
then you are caught in the frame of their
looking, sealed between two panes of
glass & you don't know what has caused
the moment to harden around you, not
this time, but then someone chuckles &
lets you pass.

//

Everyone wants to know the story of my
name. Everyone. It's a nigger joke, you
know. You already know the story. A
man is made into a thing & sutured to it.
The name.

//

There's another option. It's not the truth,
though it might be, which is, in the end,
what matters. Now, when the thing is
made to do dangerous work, he flings
its body from the low rungs of a ladder.
Limbs akimbo & fluttering & still alive.

//

Someone is talking. To you. It hardly
matters about what—their hand on your
hand & you recognize the smile. You
stutter. Mumble. Don't look them in the
eye. You fall away from the moment as if
pulled by a law governing the motion of
your body. You can't help it. You're not
in control. Give your name as proof.

//

The verb *work*. Meaning: *perform labor*
and/or *function properly.* As long as the
object works it is bound to its own
annihilation. The solution? Fall. Fall
apart. Decay.

//

Harriet wasting in the garret. The slave
caught in perpetual flight. The body
opening to receive the bullet. The
monster killing its maker & returning to
the certainty of ice.

Don't misunderstand. I don't hate white
people. Nothing here resembles hate, or
freedom from hate. *Love*, after all, *is all
you need*.

//

A nigger walks into a bar. A nigger falls
off of a ladder. A nigger is named for
its inability to function. To work. You
get the joke, right? *Awkward* as both
punishment & method. The unending
flight of *you* to *I*.

//

We haven't made it to the punch line.
Everyone is waiting. Everyone wants
resolution, for the poem to click shut.
Who gets the last word? Who, in the
end, dictates the story? I'm sorry. I really
don't know.

IN CONVERSATION WITH
CAMERON AWKWARD-RICH

Can you start off by talking about your history with writing? How and why did you get involved with poetry?

Well, like anyone, I started writing because I was a sad little kid. I mean, I had a really great life, idyllic in the most cliché American ideas about childhood. But I always felt deeply strange somehow, like I was always just adjacent to the world of other children. So, initially, I wrote in order to alleviate that sense of strangeness. Writing allowed me to invent worlds that matched my internal landscape, to invent characters who I could imagine myself as or with.

I grew up during the period in the evolution of the Internet when all kinds of message boards and the like were new and exciting, and, it seems, much more active than they are now (or maybe I have just fallen out of the world wide web). I don't know how it happened exactly, but I wound up on some creative writing message board and posted a few of these things I had been writing, and that message board almost immediately became my first literary community. It seems entirely unlike me now, but it's certainly true that the faceless strangers of the Internet were entirely responsible for my early feelings that writing was not only something I needed to do for myself, but also something I could do that other people might appreciate.

That said, I don't know how I arrived at poetry in particular. I used to write mostly fiction or short nonfiction. Maybe one explanation is that as I got older I needed elaborate fantasy worlds less and less and needed to learn to interpret the given world more and more. And that's what poetry has always done for me, allowed me to construct a frame around a bewildering experience/idea/feeling in order to hold it still long enough to begin to understand it.

In *Sympathetic Little Monster*, you openly talk about sadness. You often describe experiencing sadness in public spaces as a result of racism and transphobia. What is the role of sadness in your work, and how do you process writing about it?

Well, there are at least two answers to this question. The first is personal: I'm a fairly non-communicative person in real life. While it comes off, I think, as a kind of coldness or disinterest or wariness about intimacy (this last one is maybe true), my non-communication is often due to the fact that I have a hard time processing in the moment. I very rarely know how I feel about any given thing until I've gone through the process of putting language to it, whether by writing or talking to myself or (rarely) to someone else. So, actually, it often happens that in the process of writing I discover the emotion lurking under a particular experience or train of thought. Often, I discover sadness; it's simply the feeling to which I'm most inclined.

There is also a political or ethical answer, which is much more ambivalent. It goes something like: I think it's important to put representations out there that catalog the potentially harmful psychic consequences of racism, transphobia, sexism, and ableism. Too often, because of the existence of certain pieces of legislation and "diversity" initiatives in higher education and hiring, people believe that these are problems we've overcome and that contemporary radical/progressive activists are simply too stuck in the past or too sensitive. So, I think it's important to say that these kinds of things have real negative consequences which continue to structure our lives.

At the same time, it's also true that black sorrow and queer/trans sorrow are often consumed in ways that reinforce these systems rather than disrupt them: I can consume your sorrow in order to alleviate my guilt about being complicit in producing it, or I can view your sorrow as inherent to you rather than (potentially) the product of a system.

Either way, deadlock. So, I'm ambivalent about my own use of sadness and what it does.

I also think my writing is full of jokes! Maybe my jokes are only funny to me, but jokes are a useful navigating tool because they allow us to inhabit sorrow while laughing at it and/or to use sorrow to create protective spaces that invite a reader in if they are in on the joke.

You discuss your familial relationships in the book, especially with your dad. Has writing about your family changed your interactions with them? Do you think writing has the power to shift personal relationships?

I definitely think that writing has the power to shift personal relationships. I mean, not on its own, but writing can often provide people with the clarity they need to approach a relationship from a new angle, or to more clearly articulate what happened and what needs to change. It's a way of putting some distance between yourself and the you constituted by the relationship.

An example: I have always been my father's child, have always loved him dearly, but there were (as there always are) some things that have made our relationship rocky. I think that the degree to which I understood myself as my father's child made the bad feelings between us especially painful and difficult (for me) to interpret. It was only when I started writing about him that I was able to separate myself enough from how shitty the whole thing felt to recognize, you know, basic things. That he was a person with complex feelings and a history. That my sense of self wasn't and shouldn't be so tied to him. That even if I didn't understand or agree with many of his decisions, he made them out of a desire to make sure I was okay. That I was being a jerk.

Also, once I wrote an angsty poem about my dad and step-mom when I was still skeptical about their relationship (and then I showed it to him! Why, Cameron?!), which has become a running family joke. So there's that.

You write, "it's strange, you know, to be split. To be two things / at once." I immediately identified with this as a gender nonconforming person and thought about the ways that I am

77

pulled in many different directions. In what ways do you feel split? What can we do to not feel so fragmented in our lives?

Boy/Girl. Black/American. Black/Trans. I've felt split off from my father's side of the family by differences in class and the weird way I've always lived inside the academic world. Poet/Critic. All of the usual problems of being human in a world inevitably split by difference.

With respect to the second part of this question, I have at least two, perhaps conflicting, answers. The first answer is that one of the most important things about being a part of "like" communities is that doing so can alleviate, at least temporarily, the feeling of being split. Or, at the very least, makes that feeling manageable, because it becomes a shared feeling—a feeling that ties you to others rather than making you feel split off from them. So building these kinds of spaces and networks, formally or informally, is crucial. For lack of a better word, this is one of the reasons why intersectional thinking is so necessary, because it helps us to understand how these identities which are constructed/represented or even experienced as a conflict within us are only pitted against each other within the logic of the big systems. Capitalism. The afterlife of colonialism. On and on.

Also, I don't think feeling fragmented is necessarily a thing to seek to eliminate! Feelings, even unpleasant ones, can be a source of knowledge and intelligence. Recently I've been trying to sit with the feeling of fragmentation and ask it questions. How do these worlds/identities feel in conflict? Why? What would be gained from healing that conflict? What would be lost? Which me would survive it?

I love the way that your "Essay on the Theory of Motion" relates transness to always being in motion, rather than arriving at a fixed point. Why was motion an important subject to you?

Well, I started taking testosterone during the years in which I had just begun living in Oakland, a two-hour public transit commute away from where I go to school. Every day I would move back and forth between these two very different, very strange landscapes (Oakland with its racial/economic violence visible on the surface of everything & Palo Alto with its enormous production of racialized/classed precarity actively hidden from view). I didn't know how to navigate that disjuncture, who I was in those spaces. At the same time I felt like I was perpetually moving back and forth across some imaginary line that divided m's from f's — even now, 4.5 years later, I have a hard time predicting how I'll be gendered by others on any given day.

Like so many trans writers before me have demonstrated, the experience of gender "transition" is easily figured by tropes of travel. I was interested in being in conversation with that history because it feels important to me that there *is* a trans-literary tradition to be in conversation with, however limited. But I was also never satisfied with the travel narrative-as-transition narrative. As you point out, these kinds of narratives tend to arrive at a fixed point, gender as a knowable destination, but they also tend to be weirdly neocolonial. So I wanted to try to rewrite that trope, to see if something else could be done with it.

I have to reiterate, I was on the train a lot. Maybe too much, even.

You ask, "What is writing but the preservation of ghosts?" I think that preserving history through writing is important. I wonder if you also see your work as creating a new future in any way? Are there any writers who have helped you envision a better future?

Sure, of course. Part of the impulse to preserve history is the impulse to bring that history into the future, to make sure the good things aren't lost and the bad things aren't repeated. Also, I think of part of my work as being about creating the conditions that make it more possible for queer/trans/POC kids to live into the future. Even just in this small way of seeing themselves represented somewhere. Mostly, though, I feel very certain that the world is ending, so I am trying to leave a trace behind for the aliens.

In all seriousness, I have a hard time thinking about the future, but there are definitely people who help me to imagine it. One of the reasons I found myself drawn into the world of literary criticism/cultural studies, for example, is that so many literary critics seem so certain that art might actually provide blueprints of (or at least allow us to glimpse) better worlds. So critics like Jose Muñoz, Alison Kafer, and many other queer/crip/POC scholars are writers who have moved me toward the future. Science and speculative fiction writers have also been really important for me in this regard, especially Octavia Butler.

The one book of poems that I have to mention, though, is Ross Gay's most recent book *Catalog of Unabashed Gratitude,* which manages what is oftentimes a contradictory pull between the living and the dead and the future and the present so wonderfully. The book is so full of loss but also so full of willful creation: the work of writing, of gardening, of forging sustaining and sustainable relationships. Whew.

Lastly, what writing or art brings you joy? What is bringing you joy in your life right now?

This dovetails with the last question, but definitely the writing that brings me the most joy is that of the writers who I consider my peers: a group of mostly queer/trans and/or POC writers close to my age writing in this time and place. There are too many to name, but y'all know who you are. Sometimes their work brings me joy because it is joyous despite it all. Often their work brings me joy because of how perfectly brutal, heartbreaking, and sharp they all are. But these writers always bring me joy because it's been so gratifying to watch them succeed. I'm sure every generation has felt this way, but, all the same, it really does seem like their success is indicative of a necessary shift in the culture of American poetry. A new future.

KAY ULANDAY BARRETT

HOMEBOIS DON'T WRITE ENOUGH

homebois we don't write enough love poems.
we re-name ourselves izzie from ~~Isabella~~,
casey from ~~Cassandra~~, kay from ~~Kathleen~~.

we run out of ink for our stories cuz we've been
running through doors of male and female, never satisfied.

we stunnin' baggy jeans and bright colors over the sirens,
we stop cars and walk with a stride that makes the concrete
self-conscious about its own stability.

at the tip-toes of summer,
there you go talkin' about how you
          "need a femme pregnant and barefoot."

as I shutter asking,
          are you gonna find a stiletto ready to stab you
          if the night sticks don't come get you first?

asking—are you gonna be that bullet that is a mouth?
asking—are you gonna be that missile that blasts your woman
until she misses you, *even when you will both be in the same bed?*

if we make ourselves harder than bone,
make us a legacy that is beyond all this.

cuz I've been running through doors of male and female,
never satisfied.

that makes you nervous doesn't it?
are you worried, your palms sweaty
because I am *NOT* that kind of a man

AG
stud

butch
boi
warrior
partner
son
brother

and that might make you obsolete, that means this whole system
needs a revision. that means, we have to ask ourselves daily
are you doing your homework?

homebois, we don't write enough love poems to ourselves.
spell out our soft syllables unapologetically, letting
our strength beyond stiff jaw and cold silence,
the stuff of abandoned buildings.

let us unfold the photos with us dipped in lace and dresses and laugh
        and maybe even keep it, rejoice!
let the most tender cipher surrounding us not be our mother's tears
        for the loss of a daughter.
let us hold our breaths for the Sakia Gunns and the Fong Lee's,
        as it could easily be our sweat on this sidewalk.
let us adore the swiftness of kisses in moonlight rather than the
        pummeling cusses of strangers scared of difference.
let the tensile ace bandage be a testament across this chest,
        waving like prophets of a gender war.

let every poor black brown and yellow butch see her way into
a paintbrush, a camera, an uprock, a computer, and not into the hips of
hand grenades chucked on someone else's homeland.

to every person who squirms in the bathrooms, classrooms,
        and on stages next to me:

let them know that this moment is a clue of your queerness.
let them know my titas are at casinos burning this American dream away too
let them know my kuyas christen their kids' foreheads and give me daps
        with the same hands.

let them know that each time they make fun of us, they could be
in a feather boa, singing prince, showing their loved ones force
that will drive them toward and not away.

let their children run up and down the city as the confident trans queer kids,
who get scholarships to college for a GSA or for promoting safety at school, for
writing poems in their sickbed. (you being the backward parent they divulge to
teachers they are ashamed of.)

let me not reveal my monster each time I hear
        "I'll fuck you straight."

let my fingers not be readied trigger, grabbing sharp objects
for stabbing back.

let me walk away
without harm, disbanding my razor-edge that could
cut their lifelines, slice steel song into their temples, shear off
their pride as soon as they start to unzip their pants or call the cops.

let us know we can do this and make it clear:
we choose not to.

let us know we can do this and make it clear:
we choose not to.

homebois,
if we make ourselves harder than bone,
if we can make ourselves harder than stone,
        make us a legacy that is beyond all this.

RHYTHM IS A DANCER

Growing up, I do remember "THE ROYAL"
(pronounced like the first names "Roy" & "Al,"
for usual big gay pyrotechnics)

thursday nights as young
queers teemed in logan square
armed with body lust that could
squeeze out teenage awkward
in just one dance.

Being, in 1998, under 21, for $5
we could outwit our muscles,
discover them,
boys with eyeshadow glitz to match their
graf on avenue walls,

the pants or shirt you were forbidden
to wear at home
(due to whatever that check box
said on your birth certificate).
Our mamas probably would have
slit their wallets
if they only knew where
their work hours went.

We kissed hard.
                    We held hands.

Spoke our mother tongues
Cheek to cheek, with our *best friends*
who were really our girlfriends,
even though being 16
meant a new best friend
oh every 6 months.

Managed "it's time for the peculator,"
in the veins way before hipster
upswing tattered property taxes,
disemboweled hearts
of brown queers everywhere.

Way before white and straight folks
took our moves, bought
our clothes or put holes
in their own to call "vintage"

Some like Joanna aka Johnny,
depending if you were her father
or his lover, banished shadows with cig butts by 3am
and gave this glare like he knew
exactly how to hold you
if you needed it enough.

Or Celía who could out
pop AND lock ANY b-boy
and move her hips stunning to freestyle
swerving more than kicked snare drums.
The following morning,
girls would itch the lines of
their palms for those
angles.

Or the kids that assembled rum
and sugary juices
to forget whatever
they were or weren't coming home to.

Or the bois
who laid down their guns
at the door for a long
slow dance.

or them,

that one queer who had The Cure
and Depeche Mode buttons all over their jean jacket.
Too cool in the corner
who shook her legs a bit
particularly in appreciation of
Salt-N-Pepa, and maybe it was
a trick of the strobe lights
      but she even smirked a little.

Or us who rounded out
summer stars & sky with soprano notes.

How glorious could we have been
lodged in lockers by school day,
scared of the lies that mirrors told?

We came home breathless
from dancing our queer bodies
back to valid,
each time we'd make
a ruckus
as queer as brown
   not to reinforce stereotypes,
     but to take back the
       space that was ours.

the space in our ribcages
and in Chicago's sidewalks
that would coax us
to love.

We come from ancestors who drum and dance,
who made sweat rivulets alongside the tears
because movement had to start first on the body,
before the noose,
before the well-intended missionaries,
before the semi-automatic rifles,
before the rich studied our rhythms,

before the empty and angry,
before the straight and the narrow
beat us,

We   found   beats.

Now when I ask you,
        Giiiirrllll? What was the last jam you danced to?
        I mean reeaaallly danced to?
Sometimes I want to hear your song,
Sometimes I'll wanna listen to your beat,

But mostly
I want us to celebrate,
to honor,
to love,
to embrace,
all our movements.

ALBANY PARK/LOGAN SQUARE 1993-2000, CHICAGO, IL.

Accents, hard A's ascending on the roof of the mouth, angry and
anticipated, assembled by the air they miss all over.

Boys brandish harsh syllables, *Don't be so bakla!*
They berate. They break. They belittle until the
bright light would go barren black.
Brraaap braaap baraaap making fake
bullets into one another's brows.

Crips and Disciples. Color-clad, do's and don'ts on your clothing.
Categorize blocks a careful cartography. Caution Caution can be
cutting (among other things) come childhood.

Did I mention deep fryer sizzle as shrimp heads popPOP a firework
dance with scallions, garlic browning, adobo peppercorns flicker the
oil like summer afternoon jump rope sessions. Dinner is a dervish of
dancing dishes among cousins on tip-toes for our turn.

Elegance is a dozen expectant elders roving through a bbq,
        for balut, halo halo brazenly melted onto their soft oblong
           palms which is basically as good as prayer.

The Filipino's first call and response:
Kain na tayo! Time to eat! Food is ready! Get your asses ovah here, na!

Guaranteed commentary by a gaggle of aunties—*Ganda, no?!* gasped
over the grass grooves. Simultaneously, ghosts on ghosts in prayers
gaping on the maws of lolas gesturing rosaries.

A metallic harmony. Look, to the plastic bags heaped in hands, *can you
hold this for me, child?*

Inquiries like furtive urban inquisition:
                So when are you going to college?
                Where is your boyfriend?

Did you know—insert name—is pregnant?
going to the army?
ran away?
was locked up?

Jackfruit in spoonfuls. Jaded by the roomfuls. Jalopy speakers croon choruses of Sharon Cuneta.

Kids linked together summer nights like sutures trying to let their insides spill, sanctify the sidewalk. Kindred, feet-first,

Lolo: *Hold still will you? Look, take these flowers to your mama. Say they are from the both of us.* Leaf cutter takes a liking to the lilacs. Left languid long sprays of the hose as the old man's labor never goes unnoticed.

Miscreant: noun, [mis-kree-uh nt]
        (Migrant. Misplaced. Mapping. Misunderstood. Melancholy.)

Naturally, the bone cracks are from neighbors rushing to their night shifts or narrowly missing sunrise, packed lunches in knapsacks as they stand in the slough of gravel, a nest for feet that can never truly fly away.

Once, okay more than once / I captured glow bugs / butts blinking / in the jar a surreptitious serenade. It was like a curated collection of cosmos with a humsong, and a lid, *Hoy! What you doing?! You cannot keep creatures too long contained, they'll lose their shine!!*

P.s. did I mention? I would eat ice cream for breakfast. PPAAHHLLLLEEETTAAAA! Pulp packed on popsicle sticks, papaya, pinya,

Quezon City twang, left somewhere silky on street corners and cigarette butts, from cool kids and quips.

Roosters as alarm clocks, rake the sky with scrawled chords, loud, unforgiving.

Stoop stunners, all of us. Family be like, sacred sacred songs sung from old homelands that need salvaging. Soiled work lapels sweat ordained slack of backs hunched solemn-like. Sand daydreams in order to stay alive here in this country.

"Till tomorrow, I'll be holding you tight
And there's nowhere in the world I'd rather be
Than here in my room dreaming about you and me."
— Selena.

Upswing.
Upset.
(young mamas unimpressed by stained shirts and blurt uncomfortable internalized racisms, licking their thumbs to coat a cheek clean until it floats.)

Vexed making porches something perplex, another police officer too pleased to pound the

hips of doors til they drill whatever out of you.

Was that Tita Yoly yanking up the weeds on the corner of Albany and Waveland, in her tropical flower moomoo? Callous knees make green collisions, (she was a collector) roots yelping. It wasn't the kang kong of her riverbed, but it will have to do.

Exhaustion, for instance.

Yawning young ones. Crust-laden lids and
half-dream yammering crossing the street,
Careful careful now. You got your homework?

Sometimes indistinguishable with "S"
as in *selos* (pronounced like *zelos*),
as in jealousy.
as in what's supposed to consume you
                              when you grow up from nothing.

YOU are SO Brave.

> *& those scars i had hidden wit smiles & good*
> *fuckin*
> *lay open*
> *& i dont know i dont know any more tricks*
> *i am really colored & really sad sometimes & you hurt me*
> — *ntozake shange*

What happened? Aw, sweetie, here, let me get that for you. What do you mean "No thank you," You don't want my help? Some people are ungrateful,   I was helping YOU. You are SO brave! *Please step on the scale, Please step on the scale, Please step off the scale.* You are SO brave! I've never seen someone on a dance floor/protest move like that! What a pimp! Can I touch your cane?   *Does it hurt?*   **"People with disabilities are often seen as 'flawed' beings whose hope of normalcy rests in becoming more like non-disabled people or on becoming 'cured.'" — Sins Invalid.** (When will you get better?) Don't worry everything will be normal soon. If you just try hard enough, you will heal. If you just pray hard enough you will heal. (Have you tried acupuncture? water therapy? meditation?)   If you take these herbs enough, you can be like you were - better, normal.
Why   are   you   walking   so   slow? This is the city of the hustle, son. Buck up. If you can't speed up, leave. **Dear _____; I understand that you have accessibility needs and we as a queer progressive organization** love (love love love mmmlove) **your work but we unfortunately, we find your requests to be unrealistic. We understand that you are a queer and transgender and person of color and with limited income, but we cannot fund you at this time.** *Please do send us samples of your work so that we may distribute them to our participants   FOR FREEEEEEEEEE!* Dear *[insert assigned-at-birth name you no longer identify with that makes you want to cut yourself at every syllable];* *It has come to our attention that you are 100%*

disabled. You cannot work at all. Disabled people don't work at all. They should never work. Don't even consider working.   (Does it hurt still?)

Classification: No prolonged standing, walking, steel pin impacted osteoctomy aiken mcbride. Constant deviance in the foot based on affected use. Constant deviance. Constant deviance. Constant deviance. Cane usage to support impediment and prolonged limp.   Oh my! Look.... at that hair! Don't you have   a boyfriend to come to physical therapy with you?

"Seen as 'flawed' beings whose hope of normalcy rests in becoming more like non-disabled people or by becoming 'cured.'"

"For the report we're going to need to see some ID, [insert loud guffaw here] that cannot possibly be you. you were attractive once! What happened? Please step on the scale.   So, you were attacked? Whatdidyoudotomotivatetheattack? What exactly does LGBTQ mean? Well, Ma'am, we have to use the biological sex it says on paperwork. It'd be nice if you wore some lipstick, maybe some make up? It might make this whole process easier.   *Does it hurt still? Hasn't it been years now? Why aren't you better?* Based on your old life, don't you want to be more like me?   Heeeeeeey! Do you have a fundraiser? **I don't know any disabled people personally,** but we can raise funds to help YOU, because we think YOU deserve it. This is the city of the hustle, son. Buck up.

<u>YOU. DON'T. KNOW WHAT YOU ARE DOING!</u>

Give me that, you don't know how to take care of yourself! **Ugh, you are so slow. It's hard to imagine you could do anything yourself at all. You are so pathetic!**   (Does it hurt? Still?)

Yo homie, we're all going to the club! Should be some cuties there. Oh, yeah.... yeah, there are stairs dude. Oh yeah, sorry dude, I forgot. *The march is 2.5 miles long, maybe you can meet us at the rally?*   Aw, look at that little boy with the cane! Why do I have to get up?!#^@   **You want my seat faggot?!**   So... (long exhales) you were attacked? Why do I have to get up, chink?   Hey! I'm talking to you! Do you uh-speak uh-tha-engrrriish? **He doesn't even look disabled.**   If you have any concerns around safety at this event/conference/protest, you should really bring up these concerns with this cisgender rad skinny able-bodied person who confuses wellness work for **everybody gets better work!**   *Wait (laughs) is that supposed to be a girl?*   Awwww, you look so cute when you dance! Let me take a picture of you holding your back - *show the cane!* ***SHOWWW THE CAAANE!***   What did you do for someone to attack you? You must've done something to provoke it. Please step off the scale. You know if you lose weight, you'd be healed right?   **We'll help you because we think you deserve it,** (<u>not like some people with disabilities</u>)**,** the ones who drool and make a fuss. *Constant deviance. Constance deviance. Constant deviance.* (You'll be normal soon, won't you? Won't you?)   It's not far, just a few blocks. Aw, I know you're in pain, but you can make it, dude. What do you mean   "No thank you?"   **you don't want my help?!** *Please step on the scale,   Please step on the scale,   Please step off the scale.*

WHEN THE CHANT COMES
in gratitude for Andre Leneal Gardner

i told him what she said.
how i told her about getting top
surgery and being ready to be on T,
how my partner responded,

> do you want to be on T or get top surgery because
> you think you are fat and need to lose weight?

> how this broke me.
> it broke me.

he sucked his teeth.
a trustworthy mannerism we both got from our dead mamas.

he and I go back the way queer hungry parched kids can go way back.
back to alcoholic boyfriends

> wearing bandanas and girlfriends who
> couldn't keep their shit or dental dams together.

> > he remembered back when we were small
> > and queer and always dancing and didn't give a fuck.
> > we clocked in makeouts before cellphones scheduled
> > them for you.

brown kids ate chips from 7-11 in logan square
with deep deep house music still on their hands.
our northside and southside pride had only the pact with the
streetlamp sauntering when the club closed.

i hated my chest then.
always have.

we are no longer that young or that bold.
he's now in LA waiting tables, singing ballads like he did when we met.
he attends daily meditation sits.
he's had years of me waging this hate for my body.
my long distance news made us hold our breaths,
hold a moment of silence over phone wires.
i told him there has to be a chant for
this. he said,
baby, i'll breathe, meditate, love you,
and tell you
> *when the chant comes*

IN CONVERSATION WITH
KAY ULANDAY BARRETT

Let's start off by discussing your relationship to Chicago, which has a presence throughout *When the Chant Comes*. I picked up on various street names, neighborhoods, and references to the city. What does Chicago mean to you and how has the city influenced your life and writing?

Chicago is my epicenter. I've lived in Jersey City and worked in New York for about a decade now, but I always mention intentionally that I am a Midwestern poet and of Chi-Town. I began there, was kicked out there, started to write, became a poet and poet-educator/slam coach, led my first protest, had my first kiss, got my ass beat, worked on my first play, and became politically Queer and Brown all in the 773. I was raised in Albany Park, Logan Square, and Humboldt Park until my mid-20s, so much of my book engages in a Chicagoan sensibility and aesthetic that I cannot help but write from.

In the 90s to early 2000s I grew up in Chicago's landscape of people of color and cultural work. I was blessed to work, teach, and perform at initiatives like the first Louder Than A Bomb with Young Chicago Authors, write with the then Asian American Artists Collective, and even host events like Women OutLoud or facilitate workshops at Insight Arts. If it weren't for poets such as Lani Montreal and Tara Betts, who took time to mentor and support me, there wouldn't be a book really. This text is my own meager mapping of Chicago from a Pilipinx Queer and Trans poor kid perspective. I hope that the pages help archive some aspects of what it was like art-making in what I consider a Brown and Black poetry renaissance.

I knew where I came from: Mama Maria McCray, Patricia Smith, Sandra Cisneros, and Gwendolyn Brooks. I was taught to read and brought up by innovative writers from Chicago who were women of color. Whoever I worked with never let me forget the sacred soil where I dare lay my words. Whatever I have written, Chicago has touched it. It isn't a gross extrapolation; I do believe "I'm so Chicago…" and for that, my writing has had the bones, the training, the potlucks, and the Bulls memorabilia to prove it. Currently, there are bountiful Black and People of Color political initiatives, as well as poetry led by queers, and I cannot be anymore eternally proud of my city.

One location you mentioned in particular was the Royal, an underage club that featured a queer night in Logan Square. You write, "We came home breathless / from dancing our queer bodies / back to valid, / each time we'd make / a ruckus / as queer as brown / not to reinforce stereotypes, / but to take back the / space that is ours." Can you talk about the power of reclaiming space, how nightlife in particular provided a sense of community and belonging?

I wrote that poem in 2005. The Royal was a club where people under 21 could really shake their asses and troubles off. Located in Logan Square, with mostly Black and Brown working class youth, we were able to be ourselves whether we were in the streets, having trouble at home, working three jobs, or just looking for a queerness that played our music.

There's something magical about a dance floor and house music that will forever be salve to me. When I didn't have words for the political oppression or heartaches I faced, myself and people like me could dance it out, fuck it out, socialize it out. Of course, the drinks were expensive, the entry was inaccessible, it was an introvert's nightmare, and there would be some kind of drama, but not all of us have access to museums and institutions that embody our communities, or have places where our communities and lives are reflected. Queer club culture necessitates an alternative system of belonging when jobs, schools, systems, and institutions fail us. I could be my fullest self in nightlife, where homies spoke Spanish and had similar class backgrounds, and the music reflected our racialized lives. We could engage in our gendered and sexual selves in ways that the whiter, cis, and more affluent boystown refused to do for us.

That area is grotesquely gentrified and hardly recognizable now. I want people to have some sort of archive of their dance, night, poetry, and art spaces. I want us to remember what keeps/kept us alive when the rainbow flags and assimilation try to steamroll over the complexity of our lives.

One element of your book that I love is you have a ton of shoutouts, especially in the poem "Brown Out Shouts." You write, "we are brown and trans and queer and out / and we've been told too many times that all of those / cannot belong at once." Why did you use the shoutout as a poetic form and why is it important to name people in your work?

I believe in celebrating those who've done the work before and alongside you. Before social media and cultural capital by way of likes, we as a community had to work in ways together that were personal and messy. We had to confirm together that our work was moving forward. I think the list poem, engaged by the shoutout, isn't just specifically POC by practice, but inherently generative and unabashed. I wanted to convey, not simply respect what the people in the poem are surviving. I wanted to identify the communal power of QTPOC being listed one after another, almost like a chant.

I am frequently disturbed by the liminal space that reinforces that cis, american, white, wealthy, and able-bodied people are deserving of celebration. I want for people to have a tangible awareness that they are valid and archived in the work they are doing. From my tools, I have chosen poetry. I am concerned that QTPOC can only be honored by way of MFA, full-time jobs, and class ascension. There has to be a way we can credit one another. For those who cannot or are unable to adhere to those systems, that doesn't make them less groundbreaking. In fact, that poem is for those people. I'd venture that the solace of the shoutout is a homie-to-homie refusal for anything less than celebration and props.

"Homebois Don't Write Enough" is one of my favorite pieces in the book. It reads like a manifesto. There's a really beautiful turn in the poem where you say "homebois we don't write enough love poems… homebois, we don't write enough love poems to ourselves." You express a sense of not fitting into a binary model of gender. Can you talk more about the need to rewrite masculinity and the necessity of tenderness?

I'm so glad you appreciate that piece. There's an incessant need to rewrite and revise masculinity. There must always be room for tenderness. As a disabled and chronically-ill person of the Brown Queer masculine variety, I'm not typically what you find of the #FTM life or what people conceive of as manly. I'm personally cool by that, but that isn't the case with mainstream U.S. society. As a kid, I was for some reason on the periphery of what was considered acceptable and many times, respectable. This poem is no different.

With that as truth, I am constantly in a place of internalizing misogyny and also being a threat to the very construct itself. No matter how you have to present yourself to survive, to get that job, to be semi-respectable for food on the table, being non-binary is a hard existence and a bountiful one. For "Homebois," I wanted to stress the tension, the push and pull of battling self-love, rejoicing, being harmful, and learning lessons. Maybe it's that I wanted to push the lines to capture not only my perspective of the aesthetic of queer masculinity, but expand on its borders and bounds. It can't help but be an anthem, I'm told. It's a hymn in my heart I grapple with, that I find many homebois grapple with. It's unavoidably raced and classed. White masculinity, and in that sphere, transmasculinity, harbor such differences than my lineage and what I am and what my transiblings in my circle are. It's a man with big hips and a booty. It's a boi with sunglazed inheritance. It's the masculinity that isn't given any room on the bus to sit down when their feet are in spasms. It's the northwest side of Chicago and Bulls Starter jackets and learning multilingual Pilipinx Brown gender from migrant kuyas and grandfathers trying to get a fucking break under the Bush regimes. It's trying to hold those glories in the palms of your hands and hoping to be also something beyond what you've experienced, something better that you and the world deserve.

The piece "YOU are SO Brave" holds a mirror up to ableism and confronts it directly, along with the ways it intersects with racism, classism, transphobia, and more. What do you think the queer community can do to be more inclusive, especially of people with disabilities?

This poem is a big point of contention. In the editorial process I was actually told that this piece didn't make sense, it was confusing, and so long, and what was the point. It's a found poem, a cento, and, as someone who comes from a working-class background and as a person of color, I am accustomed to making something from scraps. I have been taught to make brilliance from heartache. The process of this poem is to make the audience work, to grapple with the scansion and with the shift in indentions and text. There's nothing cordial about ableism and the onslaught of its connections to racism, xenophobia, cissexism, fat shaming, and poverty. There's nothing clean cut or tidy. In fact it is at its best, grueling and sloppy.

What more could the queer community do? I think position Sick and Disabled Queers and Trans People's lives (as coined by Billie Rain) at the center, especially Black, Brown, Migrant, Trans, & Gender Nonconforming people. The fit and able-bodied life is temporary, y'all (Spoiler Alert!). We age and shift as human bodies. It's inevitable. We are impacted by pollutive and cruel systems that make life unlivable.

Ask yourself who isn't at your event. Basic accessibility means that you create an environment that elaborates on as many needs as possible. Everyone needs to be at the table, or honestly, your analysis is lacking and your praxis is self-aggrandizing. You can't leave people behind in these political times. Productivity is a liar and it's U.S. empire talk. Also, Google is all the rage and there are several resources out there that are guides to make your event/gathering/cultural event accessible for your participants.

You use the terms "Pilipinx" and "Pin@y" in the book--can you talk about this decision and the power of queering language?

I am coming from an American context, and I grapple with language. It's a distinct term that plays on Pinay or Pinoy, binary terms that have expressed crucial points of political and cultural necessity. I am not all feminine or masculine and many feel that these distinctions are limited in general. Again, it's about the beyond. It's about making room for the lived experiences of the "other."

The title poem of the book is so intimate and an ode to lifelong and long-distance friendship. What role has friendship played in your life, especially when so many queer and trans people turn to friends for the support their families are incapable of providing?

There's no denying when you read the text, the relationship with my family of origin is a tenuous one. If it weren't for friends, mentors, and chosen family in the development of my political and spiritual work, I am not sure where I'd be. I can't say I'd still be here, that's for sure. Friends offered me couches to sleep on when I didn't have a safe home. Friends texted me at the hospital when I acquired my disabilities. Sometimes, it's my friendships that buoy me more than anything.

I don't have the luxury or leisure to have family come by, do my laundry, and offer me food or let me crash when I need to. For some people, the sense of home has to be a nebulous one. Alternative systems of care and support are essential, yes? In that deep gap, I've had to create and build friendships that amplify whatever family means to me. In the acknowledgments of my book, every name mentioned is someone who made the book happen. Someone else's sweat brought this collection to fruition. Somebody took care of my dogs so that I could perform across the country. Another person checked access information at events to ensure my participation. Some people gave me meals when I economically wasn't at a place to do so for myself. This book wasn't written in a vacuum. It was a community investment.

I can't speak for all Queer and Trans people, but I do know the friendships that provide nourishment for a moment or for life are what have helped me to survive. I can't stress this enough: whatever you see on stage or in a poem is made possible because people believed in me and have shared their resources with my person, my being, and by proxy, my craft. Perhaps, it's the relentless Queer/Trans/Brown sorrow; how else are we supposed to live? My book's title wants to illustrate the inevitable connection you have with someone through time, whether they are breathing the same air or are thousands of miles away. What ways have we maintained roots and lineage as pushed-out peoples? As a person who lives multiple embodiments of unacceptable?

Lastly, how does it feel to finally have a book out in the world? Have you been celebrating?

I have been celebrating in small ways, though I don't feel the weight of having a book out in the world yet. I still can't believe it. The shock of when you work so hard on something and finally accomplish it is still residually there for me. In the duration of writing this book, so many people have been lost. It marks joy for me, but with this fact, also a deep sense of loss. I am elated that people are interested, buying it, and sharing it with their loved ones. My gratitude is immeasurable at this point. All I really have to say is, thank you so much for reading or for helping believe this work into existence. There's still so much more for us to write and do!

CONTRIBUTOR BIOGRAPHIES

Joshua Jennifer Espinoza is a trans woman poet living in California. Her work has been featured in *The Offing*, *PEN America*, *The Feminist Wire*, and elsewhere. Her first book *i'm alive / it hurts / i love it* was released by boost house in 2014, and her most recent collection *There Should Be Flowers* was published by Civil Coping Mechanisms in 2016.

Christopher Soto aka Loma (b. 1991, Los Angeles) is a poet based in Brooklyn, New York. He is the author of *Sad Girl Poems* (Sibling Rivalry Press, 2016) and the editor of *Nepantla: A Journal Dedicated to Queer Poets of Color* (Nightboat Books, 2018). In 2016, *Poets & Writers* honored Christopher Soto with the "Barnes & Noble Writer for Writers Award." In 2017, he was named a winner of "The Freedom Plow Award for Poetry & Activism" by Split This Rock. He frequently writes book reviews for the Lambda Literary Foundation. His poems, reviews, interviews, and articles can be found at *The Nation*, *The Guardian*, *The Advocate*, *Los Angeles Review of Books*, *American Poetry Review*, *Tin House*, and more. His work has been translated into Spanish and Portuguese. He has been invited to speak at university campuses across the country. He is currently working on a full-length poetry manuscript about police violence and mass incarceration. He cofounded the Undocupoets Campaign and worked with Amazon Literary Partnerships to establish grants for undocumented writers. He received his MFA in poetry from NYU.

beyza ozer is a queer/trans/Muslim writer living in Chicago. beyza's work has appeared in & is forthcoming from *The Offing*, *Pinwheel*, *Vinyl*, *Nightblock*, *Shabby Doll House*, and others. beyza is the author of *Fail Better* (fog machine, 2017) and *I Don't Mean to Redshift* (Maudlin House, 2016). They are deputy director of social media at YesYes Books. beyza works at Women & Children First, one of the last feminist bookstores in the country, and The Poetry Foundation.

Cam Awkward-Rich is the author of *Sympathetic Little Monster* (Ricochet Editions, 2016) and the chapbook *Transit* (Button Poetry, 2015). A Cave Canem fellow and poetry editor for *Muzzle Magazine,* his poetry has appeared in *Narrative, The Baffler, Indiana Review,* and elsewhere. Cam received his PhD from the program in Modern Thought and Literature at Stanford University.

Kay Ulanday Barrett aka @brownroundboi, is a poet, performer, and educator, navigating life as a disabled amerikan transgender queer in the U.S. with struggle, resistance, and laughter. Kay has featured at colleges and on stages globally such as Princeton University, UC Berkeley, The Lincoln Center, Queens Museum, Brooklyn Museum, and The Chicago Historical Society, to name a few, and has been invited to the White House. Currently, they are a co-host for the Mouth-to-Mouth Open-Mic Showcase at the Asian American Writers Workshop. They are a fellow of The Home School, Drunken Boat, and Lambda Literary. Their contributions are found in *PBS NewsHour,* Asian American Writers Workshop's *The Margins, Lambda Literary Review, RaceForward, Foglifter, The Deaf Poets Society, EOAGH, Poor Magazine, Fusion.net, Trans Bodies/Trans Selves, Winter Tangerine, Make/Shift, Third Woman Press, The Advocate, Buzzfeed,* and *Bitch Magazine. When The Chant Comes* is their first collection.

H. Melt [editor] is a poet and artist whose work proudly documents Chicago's queer and trans communities. Their writing has appeared many places including *In These Times, The Offing,* and *Them,* the first trans literary journal in the United States. They are the author of *The Plural, The Blurring* (Red Beard Press, 2015) and the chapbook *SIRvival in the Second City* (New School Poetics, 2013). H. Melt co-leads Queeriosity at Young Chicago Authors and works at Women & Children First, Chicago's feminist bookstore. The Lambda Literary Foundation awarded them the Judith A. Markowitz Award for Emerging LGBTQ Writers in 2017.

ACKNOWLEDGMENTS

Shout out first and foremost to *Troubling the Line,* to Trace & TC for creating the first trans poetry anthology. For opening doors and leading the way. Secondly, thank you to everyone who encouraged me when this anthology was still an idea that I didn't know how to realize: Fatimah Asghar, for our conversation on the Halsted bus and in Toni's downtown; William Johnson, for always reminding me to follow my dreams and validating me as a trans poet. Third, thank you to Bryan Borland for saying yes and all of the support and encouragement along the way. Fourth, thanks to Juan Felipe Herrera and Ari Banias for their support. It's been a joy to work with both of you. Of course, thank you to Joshua Jennifer Espinoza, Christopher Soto, beyza ozer, Cameron Awkward-Rich, and Kay Ulanday Barrett for leading us into the future. To all trans people, poets, and writers, we're here and we're not going anywhere.

Many of these poems were originally published in the following collections:

There Should Be Flowers by Joshua Jennifer Espinoza, Civil Coping Mechanisms, 2016.

Sad Girl Poems by Christopher Soto, Sibling Rivalry Press, 2016.

Fail Better by beyza ozer, Fog Machine, 2017.

Sympathetic Little Monster by Cameron Awkward-Rich, Ricochet Editions, 2016.

When the Chant Comes by Kay Ulanday Barrett, Topside Press, 2016.

In addition, the below poems and interviews appeared in the following publications:

American Poetry Review: "[Somewhere in Los Angeles] This Poem is Needed" & "Self Portrait as Sonoran Desert" by Christopher Soto.

Indiana Review: "Still Life" by Cameron Awkward-Rich.

Lambda Literary: Interviews with Cameron Awkward-Rich & Kay Ulanday Barrett.

Literary Hub: "All the Dead Boys Look Like Me" by Christopher Soto.

Tin House: "In Support of Violence" by Christopher Soto.

Vinyl Poetry & Prose: Interview with Christopher Soto.

ABOUT THE PRESS

Sibling Rivalry Press is an independent press based in Little Rock, Arkansas. It is a sponsored project of Fractured Atlas, a nonprofit arts service organization. Contributions to support the operations of Sibling Rivalry Press are tax-deductible to the extent permitted by law, and your donations will directly assist in the publication of work that disturbs and enraptures. To contribute to the publication of more books like this one, please visit our website and click *donate*.

Sibling Rivalry Press gratefully acknowledges the following donors, without whom this book would not be possible:

TJ Acena	JP Howard	Tina Parker
Kaveh Akbar	Shane Khosropour	Brody Parrish Craig
John-Michael Albert	Randy Kitchens	Patrick Pink
Kazim Ali	Jørgen Lien	Dennis Rhodes
Seth Eli Barlow	Stein Ove Lien	Paul Romero
Virginia Bell	Sandy Longhorn	Robert Siek
Ellie Black	Ed Madden	Scott Siler
Laure-Anne Bosselaar	Jessica Manack	Alana Smoot Samuelson
Dustin Brookshire	Sam & Mark Manivong	Loria Taylor
Alessandro Brusa	Thomas March	Hugh Tipping
Jessie Carty	Telly McGaha & Justin Brown	Alex J. Tunney
Philip F. Clark	Donnelle McGee	Ray Warman & Dan Kiser
Morell E. Mullins	David Meischen	Ben Westlie
Jonathan Forrest	Ron Mohring	Valerie Wetlaufer
Hal Gonzlaes	Laura Mullen	Nicholas Wong
Diane Greene	Eric Nguyen	Anonymous (18)
Brock Guthrie	David A. Nilsen	
Chris Herrmann	Joseph Osmundson	

CPSIA information can be obtained
at www.ICGtesting.com
Printed in the USA
FSHW010426130320
67985FS